Oceans of Thoughts

Book Two

A Wave Of Smooth Intensity, Captivating Energy, And

A Historical Movement Of A Musical Decade

To:
John
PR From the
HEART

Do Enjoy Reading
this Book Series
Oceans of thoughts
thanks for your
support

Rosalind McClean
3/16/2022

Rosalind Severin McClean

Oceans of Thoughts

Copyright © 2021 Rosalind Severin McClean

Cover photography by Pawan Kumar

Logo illustration by Rene Y. Sumagang

Printed in the United States of America

ISBN: 978-0-578-93710-6

Dedication

I am dedicating Oceans of Thoughts: Book Two to the members of the Missin' Dimensions Band of the 1970s. I feel honored to have documented the journey of DE BAND, and to share the history with everyone. I would also like to thank them for the exceptional memories of this historical phenomenon which we created in Dominica (DA).

All Biblical quotes come from the authorized (King James) version

TABLE OF CONTENTS

Acknowledgments

I have devoted my attention to bringing forth to you another book in this series, and now I have finally completed Oceans of Thoughts: Book Two. I would like to extend my appreciation to everyone who has supported and encouraged me along this journey, including:

my daughter Malti McClean for her computer skills and expertise; Jennifer Fadelle Johnson who has been very influential on the process especially on the project of DE BAND; my nephew Garvin Richards; members of my team for their commitment; and my coach for his confidence.

I would also like to thank the following people for their photo contributions: Gordon Henderson, Albie Frampton, Brian Rock, Levi Loblack, Desmond Green, Worrel Hurtault, Jeffrey Fadelle and the members of the Missin' Dimensions Band.

I thank you all.

Rosalind Severin McClean

OCEANS OF THOUGHTS

The Preternatural Mind

Blessings All!

As I sit in the frame of mind to carve Oceans of Thoughts: Book Two, I gravitate to all the positive energies that stream through this mediation.

Jah Bless this awe-inspiring journey of Oceans of Thoughts through His mighty power of being.

Jah Bless this wave of Oceans of Thoughts as He pulsates on the balance of consciousness.

Jah Bless this intriguing movement of Oceans of Thoughts as He penetrates through the focus of thought.

It is the preternatural mind of creation that prints the perfection in the imperfections on the canvas of life as nothing is perfect, just as it is the reverse stamp of intervention that prints the unappreciations in the appreciation of written word in poetry, that translates to song in music.

I remain thankful for the testimony of His script on my work for it is only by that mission I write.

I remain grateful for He has polished this artistry of speech through poetry in the inspiration shown to me.

I look to Jehovah Shalom as I transcribe the vision of His creative design in the messages of Oceans of Thoughts.

"I will praise thee; for I am fearfully and wonderfully made: marvelous are thy works" (Psalm 139:14)

"I have more understanding than all my teachers for thy testimonies are thy meditation" (Psalm 119: 99 [Mem])

"The word is a lamp unto my feet, and a light unto my path" (Psalm 119:105 [Nun])

OM to the greatest Shalom for the Lord is Peace that stills the mind of wisdom.

OM to the genius of the Creation of plenty that drips the nectar of knowledge.

OM to the Omnificent One, the director of Oceans of Thoughts.

Om Namah Shivaya!

Namaste!

-- Rosalind Severin McClean, March 11, 2021

Introduction

Yes! I am excited to present to you Book Two of my *Oceans of Thoughts* series.

Book Two is another conscientiously written book of poetry written in lyrical and dialect writing styles. It is an inspirational journey of life which penetrates through your thoughts and holds you true to your emotions.

The variations reflected in my writing correlate with all who read my work and hear about it. The many reviews shown to *Oceans of Thoughts* are a testament to the impact that my work has on everyone.

Also, in Book Two, I grip you along the thrilling experiences of the Missin' Dimensions Band of the 1970s in Dominica (DA).

I encourage everyone to read Book Two and to join me on the wonderful journey of *Oceans of Thoughts*. This book is sure to captivate your interest.

I thank you all for supporting my work.

INNOCENCE

Preface

This beautiful masterpiece is a true witness to the transparency of the separations of life on the emotions of childlike innocence.

It is a brilliant display of the effects of Cosmic energies through Divine Intervention on a tender life of six.

Its lyrics flow through two peduncles of art.

Come along with me as we drift on the sweet inspiring incense of the lilies of life.

-- Rosalind Severin McClean, April 23, 2021

"The jewel in the heart of the lotus
is symbolical of the soul within man
which reflects God's
eternal splendor and perfection."

-- NORVELL

THE RIVERBANKS

On the riverbanks
Of Divine Intervention
Radiant pools of dazzling waters
Reflections of brilliant sunlight
Mirrors of celestial blue skies
Adorning cliffs of coral yellow
A yellow of cosmic sight
A scenery of immaculate perfection
A dream spread of far dimensions

On the riverbanks
Of Divine Intervention
Dripping with fountains
Of love and sweet sensations
Six incense lilies of life
Bubbling in the silvery waters
Embracing in precious moments
Floating over tranquil currents

Six incense lilies of life
In gentle transparent imaginations
Blowing kisses in the winds
Cherishing simple childish moments
Drifting in simple childish fantasies
Holding truth to trust profound

Afloat on Divine Intervention
Six incense lilies of life
Crafting healthy smiles and chatter
Splashing in playful manner
Drifting on the riverbanks
Of Divine Intervention

Grey shadows peep
Over the silvery waters
Hazy clouds suddenly appear
Unforeseen crystal storms
Unsuspecting passion wilts
Innocence emotions shatter
Childlike expectations wimp
Childhood securities torn
Shifting in the shadowed waters
Of awaiting expectations
On the riverbanks
Of Divine Intervention

Amidst the tempest
Of Divine Intervention
Six incense lilies of life
Aplomb bundle of silk
Lustrous white in the haze
Weaved on stems of crochet

Six incense lilies of life
Levitating in the air
Meditating in perfect oneness
Above turbulence of unnatural waves
Soaked in rains of crystal droplets
Through the woven passing storm
A testimony exhibited
Of atmospheric change
Oversaturated with the ether
Of Divine Intervention

****

Welcome rays of sunshine
Peeping through white clouds
High above in four dimensions
Of magnificent celestial skies

Six incense lilies of life
Survival of the mysterious storms
Awakening bright from meditation
More breathtaking in perfection
More inspirational in creation
More mystical in scenic beauty

Six incense lilies of life
Survival of the mysterious storms
Slowly absorbing new abundance
Breathing sweet, assorted perfumes
Embracing the miracle of life
Of the adorning cliffs of coral yellow
On the riverbanks
Of Divine Intervention

Blossoming in harmonious cluster
Six incense lilies of life
Smoothly drifting over dazzling waters
Rains of clear crystal droplets
Running off its gentle petals
In the calmness of the wind

Six incense lilies of life
Triumphant on accord
Pulsating music of pure chimes
Strumming from flawless petals
In the dance of melodious rhythms
Six incense lilies of life
Sharing accolades of cosmic bliss
Spreading kisses of new life
Resplendent of nature's craft
Victorious over the storms
On the riverbanks
Of Divine Intervention

As one gazes at the open cosmos
And its most majestic creation
One is drenched in appreciation
Of its most magnificent nature

The rhymes of creation
The rhymes of challenge
The rhymes of change
Plentiful in nature

Six incense lilies of life
Meditating on the oneness
Transcending through the grace
Levitating through the space
In gentle transparent imaginations
Over pools of dazzling waters
Over pools of dazzling waters
On the riverbanks
Of Divine Intervention

Om Namah Shivaya!

-- Rosalind Severin McClean, August 7, 2020

SPIRITUAL

Preface

As I ponder and write the lyrics of this poem, I see even more clearly the misinterpretations and the misunderstandings of the presence of the Messenger in our circles.

The futile discussions and whispers steam through three stems in the space of the silence.

The atmosphere is saturated.

I look to the great inspiration of the Ancient Muses to direct this dialogue.

-- Rosalind Severn McClean, April 24, 2021

"It is easy to see the faults of others,
but difficult to see one's own faults.
One shows the faults of others like
chaff winnowed in the wind,
but one conceals one's own faults as
a cunning gambler conceals his dice."

-- THE DHAMMAPADA

THIS IS A NEW DAY! OR, IS IT?

Patterned on the belief that
Every being perceives life
Fashioned in his own way
The misuse of his own intellect
Capsizes the invisible balance
Of intelligent focus
Which throbs directly through
The curious minds
On the contrary
Their own intelligence
Opposes them

Steams of antipathetic energies
Muttered intently
In the fabricated quietness
Amidst the social circle
The large black cauldron
Sizzled with vigor
In the ear-piercing stillness
Uncharacteristic vacuity
Sigh!
This is a new day!
Or, is it?

Spoken through shades
On the colorful canvas
The surface of
That impressive painting
Bled!

The impact of the artistry
On this awe-inspired figure
Closets of imagination
Overshadowing that painting
The loud unmarked silence
Oozed!

Those melted oily mixtures
Splattered unanticipated dots
Captivating that painted canvas
The wisdom of that artistry
Soared!
This is a new day!
Or, is it?

****

Like infected open sores
Harvesting porous flesh
Worthless cultivated attitudes
Soaked in that cauldron pot

Those huge wooden spoons
Stirring unhealthy whispers
Seasoned with hypocrisy
Of honesty dishonesty
Exhaled cautiously
Through those vibrating cracks
This is a new day!
Or, is it?

Curved feathered weakness
Rich in acceptance of
Risen flares of perspectives
Defining convenient appreciations
Of lyrical art

An educated guess
Sunk in the deafening silence
Abass the midnight air

The message missed
The Messenger unnoticed
Fallen through the deafening quiet
Streamed from the center
Of that circled air

Unweathered particles shifted
Through spoken word
Coup d'œil
Evaporated through that massive
Black boiling cauldron pot
This is a new day!
Or, is it?

****

Brilliant emerald gem
Blossomed in the scarlet night
Rotating freely on that
Enormous zodiac orbit

Accelerated on endless vision
The honored emerald stone
With unstoppable talents
Gifted to inspire
And natural at best
Pellucid!
Balanced on karma
Incredible!
The nature of balance
Does it ever function?
This is a new day!
Or, is it?

Empowered in the opulence of
The universal space of the arts
The figure on that painting
Revealed through the wisdom
Of the unending universe
Rotating on the axis of
Space in time unmeasured

Dignity and gratitude
To the rich influences
And limitless talents
Of the great Muses
Of the Ancient ages
The Greek goddesses
Of poetic inspiration
Of lyric and of epic
Of song and of art

The hot cauldron steams
Overflowing with Divine purposes
Oversaturated with Divine gifts

Served! In the transparency
Of the magnificent plan
And virtuous principles

Served! In the clarity
Of boundless interpretations
And understandings

And
Served! In the revelations of
The power of the messages
And the goodness without limit
Of
The Omnipresent One

This is a new day!
Or, is it?

Om Namah Shivaya!

Namaste! Peace

-- Rosalind Severin McClean, January 31, 2021

OCEANS OF THOUGHTS

Preface

In a moment of pure bliss and infinite forgiveness, the realization of the loss of three cycles of life surfaced.

Inexplicable to the utmost.

This poem initiates the influences and patience to reunite these lost years to the victorious end.

I computed this inspirational poem in four parts to document this phenomenal lifetime experience.

-- Rosalind Severn McClean, April 24, 2021

"The infinite in man longs for the Infinite.
The love that moves the stars also moves the heart of man,
and a law of spiritual gravitation leads his soul
to the Soul of the universe."

-- JUAN MASCARO

UNEXPLAINED ABSENCES

In the midst
Of the awakening
Of the Full Moon
Glowing brilliantly
Propitious and clear
Waves of telepathy
Flowing through
The tranquil night

The extraordinary stir
Caressing in superlative
Extrasensory perception
In the revelations
Of perplexed
Unexplained absences

In the bosom
Of her gentle spirit
Nudging spur
Qualities untainted
Mind transient
Wrapped in clusters of
Droughts of turmoil

Unbeknownst
Hidden
In the shades
Of questionable
Unexplained absences

Her sweet aura
Equanimous energies
Roaming through clouds
Beyond her reach
Equable personalities
Magnetic pneuma
Admired by many

Fluorescence
Windows of smiles
Overflowing on those
Unknown inquires
Hushed
In the shadows
Of puzzling
Unexplained absences

Bounced on bundles
Of perfumed cushions
Of her lilac essence
Unnatural resources
Inevitable
Belief yet disbelief

Delightful bright flavors
Faithful on sight
Passive
Streams of ages
Brushed
Belief yet disbelief

Shifting on hopes
Gentle breeze
Falling steadily through
Protective cracks
Amidst her joys
Subtle
Belief yet disbelief

Engrossed
In that knot of
Self-entanglement
Preserved
In the myth of
Self-searching
Through
That empty space
Belief yet disbelief

Reaching nowhere
Not a clue
Deep amid oceans
Of quivering thoughts
Of inconceivable
Unexplained absences

Three life cycles
Drifted slowly away
Whispering twenty-one
On humble ground
Searching endlessly for
Mysterious purposes
Of
Those reflective
Unexplained absences

RISEN THOUGHTS

In the glorious light
Of the magnificence
Of the Full Moon
Her beautiful persona
Prestigious on art
Danced to the beat
Of the lightning bug's
Creative flirt

Wishful golden ideas
Wandering with no grip
Movements of glistening
Veracious cautious tips
Encouraging

Embracing tunes
On the bass rhythm
Of her heartbeat
Melody in song
Patience

Cascading through
The twin waterfalls
Of her humility
God's timing
Always on point
Contemplating

Completing her journey
Of risen thoughts
Surprising
Gratifying
He knew
Her confidante

THE SPIRIT OF THE MOON

Burst of ineffable relief
Full of mystic sensations
Pulsating blissfully
Through
The spirit of the Moon

Creations of ecstasy
Levitating through
Cherished moments
Of laughter on confession

The luminous glow
Of the Silver lining
Reflecting gracefully
Through
The spirit of the moon

Three life cycles
Free!
Lost in colorful
Unspoken detachments
And
Unmentioned pain

Suppressed vividly in
The absolute mystery
Of
The spirit of the moon

Those lost years
Twenty-one shown
Never!
To be returned

THE MEDITATION

In the roaming
Of brilliant energies
Of the gravitating pulse
Of the Full Moon
Shattered icy formations
Through infinite hints
Of
The spirit of the Moon

Cracking miraculously
Orchestrated
The pleasant tone of
Her warm casual hello
Spoken softly
In honest confession

In the meditation
Of the thankfulness
Of cosmic expressions
Ice cubes of empathy
Spinning on trust
Genuine friendships
With mended hearts
And lifetime joys
Harmoniously evolve

Heaps of crushed ice
Gracefully melted away
Fulfilling the mystery
In the levitations
In Divine mediation
Purifying
And
Transcending those
Unresolved Ministries
Of
Unexplained Absences

OM!
To the Limitless
The Lord and Creator
Of love
Of the Universe
The Author of Life
And the Finisher
The EL-ROI[1]
The strong One who sees
The strong One who sees

Namaste!

JAH Bless!

-- Rosalind Severin McClean, December 27, 2020

---

[1] "The strong one who sees" Genesis 16:13

INTENSE

Preface

As asked in Reflective Meditations:

"What is the quality of your thoughts?

Can you determine when your thoughts are constructive or destructive?

Can you watch that destructive thought while it is in the making?

If so, can you reconstruct that energy to one that is beneficial?"

I was prompted to write this piece which exhibits those thoughts of the untrained ego.

-- Rosalind Severin McClean, April 25, 2021

"This above all: to thine own self be true,
And it must follow, as the night the day,
Thou canst not then be false to any man."

WILLIAM SHAKESPEARE, "Hamlet"

OH GASP! HE SAID NO

Glowing orange shadows
Perpetuate desiring minds
Confuse impecunious hearts
And anxiously fabricate

Searching and waiting
Through uneasy waters
Surfing deep waves
Through courageous
Tedious long swims

Strength valiantly prevails
Continuous efforts win
Complicated
Intricate
Lack and weep
Oh gasp!
He said no

Waves of thoughts
In survival mode
Stretch and yearn
In desperate measure

Oh! Praiseworthy moon
Oh! Infinite expansion
Of shining silvery light
Of far reach
Of far sight
Stretch and yearn
Mystic favored pressures
Oh gasp!
He said no

Empty words flooded
That fibber's mouth
Hopeful truth propelled
Thrust straight through
Such perfidious
Spoken wonder

Callous rapid bluffer
Demonstrating no trust
Beguiled solid pride
Self-centered talker
Displaying characteristics
Egotistic
Egocentric
Phony

Sincere hearts filled
But mistakenly engrossed
Honest emotions crushed
Oh gasp!
He said no

Carry on, champ
With that boastful ego
Flaunting bravery
Wealthy personality
Procrastinating
Self-absorbed
Self-obsessed
And painfully wrong

No compassion
No empathy
No honesty
Oh gasp!
He said no

Honor and majesty
Pulsating in superior motion
Show absolute humility
In the dance of
Rhythmic emotion

Show thyself
Thy favored sponsor
Thy greatest provider
Thy kindest giver
Thy selfless contributor
Oh! Jehovah Jireh[2]

Smile and shine
Amidst the open
Glowing orange curve
Streams of overflow await
Stand firm and stand strong
On solid favored ground

Oh! Daughter of Shammah[3]
Oh! Daughter of the Universe
Carefully encompassed and
Mystically saturated
In positive vibrations
Of Divine Creation

Oh! Daughter of Light
Oh! Daughter of Thought
Absorb those orange waves
Of positive currents
Soak in the energies
Of optimistic flow

---

[2] "The Lord will provide" Genesis 22"13-14
[3] Jehovah Shammah: "The Lord who is present" Ezekiel 48:35

Glowing orange beam
Pulsating through
Abundance of light
In pure consciousness

Oh! Daughter of Nature
Oh! Daughter of Nurture
Strength radiantly prevails
Continuous efforts win

Spin it around
And tightly suppress
That distressful sound
Oh gasp!
He said no

OM! To the Greatest Provider

Om Santih Santih Santih! Peace!

Namaste!

-- Rosalind Severin McClean, June 28, 2014

Preface

I was propelled to craft this poem as an instrument to clip the wings of the Silent Bully;

That silence, a psyche of the bully that is not so easily detected, therefore, is always denied and is difficult to correct.

This very unkind behavior is experienced by just about everyone from childhood throughout life.

I meditated on the Spirit of Proverbs to pen the intensity of this social oppression.

I recited this poem at a few events and each time the audience was voiceless.

"He that walketh upright walketh surely: but he that perverteth his ways shall be known" (Proverbs 10:9)

-- Rosalind Severin McClean, April 24, 2021

"Happy the man who discovers wisdom,
the man who gains discernment:
gaining her is more rewarding than silver,
more profitable than gold."

-- PROVERBS 3:13 (Jerusalem Bible)

THE SILENT BULLY

Fluid excitement

Pleasured mistreatment

Mistaking kindness for weakness

Scheming ploy

Sneaking!

Contentious conspiracy

Deceptive!

Miscreant!

Secret mesh

Of the Silent Bully

Pretense amity

Smile and greet

Common courtesy

Ethics misfit

Pretense amity

Hypocrites meet

Spitefully cunning

Giggle, laughing feat

Pretense amity

Shrewd!

Unforeseen mesh

Of the Silent Bully

Blatant disrespect
Congregating near
Boldly ostracizing
Showing no fear
Revengeful demeanor
Expressing!
Hand spanking
Underneath!

Midday ordering
Midway grouping
Distastefully brave
Controlling!
Unidentified mesh
Of the Silent Bully

Boisterously mesmerizing
Social butterfly
Mockingly spitefully sly
Frantic, morning display
Transparent guilt
Shameful!

Deaf ears could hear
Blind eyes could see
Unsuspecting misconduct
Perversely corrupt
Mischievous mesh
Of the Silent Bully

Furious manipulator
Fashioned protected power
Prevaricated conference
Incited boastful
Retaliatory behavior
Retaliatory behavior!
Unresolved!

Still that play!
No more, no more! Annihilate
Holy Spirit intercede for me
Even if I can't say what I want to say
Still that play!
No more, no more! Desegregate
Refrain, regain, respect plain
Still that play!

Revel purity inner peace
Revel purity inner strength
No more, no more! Envious masquerade
Oh Lord!
Eradicate that undercover mesh
Of the Silent Bully

Proverbs:
When pride comes, then comes shame,
But with the humble is wisdom
The integrity of the upright will guide them
But the perversity of the unfaithful will destroy them
The righteous should choose his friends carefully
For the way of the wicked leads them astray
The wisdom of the prudent is to understand his way
But the folly of fools is deceit
He who walks with the wise man will be wise,
But the companion of fools will be destroyed

Peace!
Great OM!
Repudiate that Secret mesh
Of the Silent Bully
Peace!

-- *Rosalind Severin McClean, May 16, 2018*

LIGHTHEARTED

Preface

I wrote this very cheerful poem inspired by cell phones and the effects of internet interruptions, in the middle of a busy rush hour.

It is written with a slight dialect using 'de' for the.

I have recited this poem at Open Mic events and the responses that flooded through were so encouraging. The audiences were absolutely humored.

Do enjoy this train ride with me.

-- Rosalind Severin McClean, April 23, 2021

"It is not thought we should want to know:
we should want to know the thinker."

-- KAUSHITAKI UPANISHAD

AND YOU!

And You!
Smile a pleasant mask
In anticipation
Of a sure communication
Via de cell phone
Yet text
Yet calls
Not shown

And you!
Stare with intent
Not to mock
Not to pretend
Yet you focused
Forehead intense
Hum!
De blank screen
Unknown

And You!
Smile a pleasant mask
In this mystical place
In an empty space

Eyes fixed on de buff
None stop
No internet
No connection

Still!
Fingers clicking
Eyes, shying glancing
From side to side
Yet! No one looking
At de cell phone
Blank
Lock screen face

And You!
Smile a pleasant mask
In this faithful plight
Grasping!
De cell phone tight
Scrolling through
Old scanty messages
On WhatsApp site

Still!

Fingers clicking

Eyes, shying glancing

From side to side

A spark

A glee

But!

Nothing new!

Nothing new

****

And You!
Smile a pleasant mask
Eyes transfixed
On de electric clock
De rush tight
Stressed and might
De subway trains
Energies strained
Yet no internet
No! Not yet

A yearning chant
From deep within
Memories of old
Worthy to be told
Reflecting through
That!
Well of gold

Yet!
Fingers clicking
Eyes, shying glancing
From side to side
In that nest!
In that nest

And You!
Smile a pleasant mask
To fit in
De massive crowds
Of
De internet mobs
Constant texting
Video, vlog and calling

But you!
In that dense embrace
Perplexed thoughts race
Your pending messages
Yet to come
No data
No internet
No! Not yet

Still!
Fingers clicking
Eyes, shying glancing
From side to side
But nothing!
Nothing at all

And You!

Yes you

Smile a pleasant mask

In beams of flickers of light

In streams of extending sight

In moments of wishful delight

Imagining!

Yes! Imagining

When your messages come

But!

You are stranded

So! Stranded

In this internet plight

Still!

Fingers clicking

Eyes, shying glancing

From side to side

You're not alone!

You're not alone

And suddenly!

Commuters exclaim

In excitement

An internet correction
All cell phones connection
And buffering no more
Fascinating!

Internet mobs indulge
Messaging, video, vlog and calling
Inspiring inspirational settling vibes
Brushing through de massive crowds
Uttering praises on de spirit OM
Holding de cell phones in their hands
In complete satisfaction

And then!
You smiled that victorious smile
Shared with the internet mobs
You web your way
Intently through
Those eager internet crowds
To your trusted destination
Relieved!
Rejuvenated
In absolute exhilaration

And you!
Smiled a pleasant mask

Peace!

-- Rosalind Severin McClean, February 22, 2018

OCEANS OF THOUGHTS

DE BAND

DE BAND: 1970-1977

Part 1

Blessings all!

It has been an amazing journey of writing. I am incredibly grateful for the continuing flow of support from everyone. Thank you for reading and enjoying my writing style.

I was listening to a group of high school teens playing pop music at a concert in the park. This lit up a memory chord of my high school days in music. I became so exuberant that I knew then it was time to share some experiences of my music background and history.

OM to the Most High for His Divine guidance and His protection on my writing style. Peace!

-- Rosalind Severin McClean, May 30, 2019

Preface

This series of seven poems on DE BAND is written with a slight twist of the Dominican (DA) dialect, using 'de' for 'the' and 'dey' for 'they.'

Part 1 is written to emphasize the DUO partnership on acoustic guitars.

-- Rosalind Severin McClean, December 2, 2012

"If ever your life is out of tune,
And no music soothes the soul,
Seek out The Master whose gentle touch
Will bless you and make you whole."

-- KEN BROWN

DE VERY BEGINNING OF "THE MISSIN' DIMENSIONS BAND" THE DUO

We first started off
In de early 1970s era
Jennifer and Rosalind
Playing our box guitars
To folk tunes for
Dr. Edward Watty's folk group
Dominica's famous Goodwill Singers

Sold out concerts
They were
At de Saint Gerard's Hall
With de famous Goodwill Singers
Performing to great songs
Like 'Sloop John B'
Which will never be forgotten
By our Jennifer
Under strict instructions
And she could never get it
To play with a 'zing'
As the 'Doc' called it

Night practices at his house
Was a bountiful must
Yet!
Not to complain
As de final product
Which will
Always be remembered
Aroused a full house

De phenomenal shows began
With stunning performances
Overwhelming audiences
Beautiful singing
Great acting and
Our captivating highlight
De accompaniment of
Our box guitars

We played that music
And strummed de box guitars
Throughout those grand performances
We became famous too
Being known as
De DUO
Sitting in full view
At de corner of
De performing stage

Of course
A standing ovation
From over-enthusiastic crowds
At each grand show
Compliments to de fullest
To de proud guitarists
Jennifer and Rosalind
Of Dr. Watty's masterpiece

First Band Members on acoustic guitars:

Rosalind Severin McClean
Jennifer Fadelle Johnson

-- Rosalind Severin McClean, December 2, 2012

DE BAND: 1970-1977

Part 2

Preface

This series of seven poems on DE BAND is written with a twist of the Dominican (DA) dialect, using 'de' for 'the' and 'dey' for 'they.'

Part 2 is written to highlight the members of our Convent High School Band.

-- Rosalind Severin McClean, December 2, 2012

*"Music and rhythm find their way
into the secret place of the soul."*

-- PLATO

CONVENT HIGH SCHOOL BAND

In this amazing
1970s era
As we continue on
We formed DE BAND
We had no name
But just
Norlda, Ella, Jean, Jennifer and Rosalind

At that time
Back in rolling 1971
Of our blissful
Convent High School days
School to de music
Instruments in sight
De electric guitars were it

Some Belgium nuns[4]
So graciously fulfilling the need
Of electrical music instruments
For a Convent High School Band

---

[4] Refers Belgian nuns

Rose Caines as singer
Jennifer and Rosalind on electric guitars
Rosalind alternating to de organ
Norlda running de bass
Ella and Jean on de drums

Slamming we were
With great hits in de days
Pop and religious music
Songs like 'Venus'
Songs like 'Oh Happy Day'
Songs like 'Day after Day'
Songs like 'Hang on Snoopy'
Songs to name a tune

Music playing
Strings bursting
Drums banging
'Venus' was she name
Jennifer playing hard
Vexed at de song
Oh boy!
Pop went
Those metal guitar strings

Convent High School concerts
Housed at
The Goodwill Parish Hall
The grand Saint Gerard's Hall
Not in use
Oh well!
Wherever we played
We rocked the house

Awe-inspiring
And entertaining we were
In de 1970s era
All schoolgirls and boys
Teachers, Nuns and Christian Brothers
And other curious and excited fans
Packed in a screaming
Goodwill Parish Hall

A vivacious Miss Cools-Lartigue
School teacher on popular seat
Saint Mary's Academy production
Made full request
On demand
To play at
The all-boys high school
SMA yearly school fair

A burst of our performing grace
Pulling de mesmerized crowd
With more and more
Exhilarated and fascinated fans
To add to DE BAND
Growing music repertoire

DE BAND Members (Convent High School Band):

Rosalind Severin McClean
Jennifer Fadelle Johnson
Rosalind Caines Laroque
Arnolda Williams Shillingford
Ella Butler
Jean Munro (R.I.P.)

-- Rosalind Severin McClean, December 2, 2012

DE BAND: 1970-1977

Part 3

Blessings all!

Grace to you and peace from God our Father and Lord, the Alpha and the Omega, Jah!

I am channeling my healing energy to keep this wonderful writing project flowing, and to bring forth this energy to my many supporters on this Oceans of Thoughts project.

It is true that the gift of poetry is not appreciated by some; however, everyone to his own likeness.

But, to my many supporters on this great project of writing, and to all the new ones coming along, I extend my gratitude to you. Salutations to the OM, who is the greatest Provider of all.

Peace!

Preface

This series of seven poems on DE BAND is written with a twist of the Dominican (DA) dialect, using 'de' for 'the' and 'dey' for 'they.'

Part 3 is written to draw attention to some of the struggles we faced as female musicians needing electric instruments and practice space.

-- *Rosalind Severin McClean, December 2, 2012*

"Music can change the world."

-- BEETHOVEN

GROWING POPULARITY

We continue on
In the 1970s era
Where religion
And music compete
As we climbed up on
De heat of de music
We unwittingly
Broke away from
De Convent School electric music

Sister José, 'de spider'
As we called her
Principal of the Convent High School
Opposed to our burst
Of playing pop music
At our minimal venues
Of our music interest
Sister José
Subsequently cancelled
Our practice sessions
In the Convent High School Hall

Well!
De madam stepped in
Mrs. Celia Fadelle
Defending our plea
Of playing trendy music
Choice of de day's hits
Of pop melodies

De Liquid Ice Band
Became our refuge
For band practice
And electric instruments
In de Fadelle's cellar
That move created
A melting ground
And a racket of confusion

"No," dey opposed
"Yes," we charged
With Mr. Fadelle to our rescue
"Dey playing," he put down his foot
"Or, you are not," was his command

Victory was ours
DE BAND in full swing
Attracting all de neighbors
And boys and girls from afar
And other hangout crew
De crowd always thick
Congregating outside
By de Fadelle's house
To get a piece of de action

Liquid Ice Band members well vex
We conquered their space
Mickey, Glen, Marcus, Sty
And sweet Tony too
All in grumbling defeat

DE BAND well-formed
No name to boast
Searching our brains
We did
To make DE BAND formal
Tapping in her creative mind
Came Rosalind's best
With
"DE MISSIN' DIMENSIONS"

That's how it started folks
We made history in Dominica, DA
"De Missin' Dimensions"
Is de name
Of our music reign
The first all-girl group
On electric instruments
On de island Dominica, DA
And the entire Caribbean
Ever formed is
"De Missin' Dimensions"

French tourists on the island
Embraced us with invitations
All expenses paid
To perform
In near
Guadeloupe and Martinique

Barbados TV[5] and
Saint Lucia TV[6] too
Wanted an interview
But, "no way"
Mrs. Fadelle and
Mrs. Severin say
"De Missin' Dimensions"
In Dominica, DA to stay

DE BAND Members ("De Missin' Dimensions"" Band):

Rosalind Severin McClean
Jennifer Fadelle Johnson
Arnolda Williams Shillingford
Ella Butler
Jean Munro (R.I.P.)

-- Rosalind Severin McClean, December 2, 2012

---

[5] Caribbean Broadcasting Corporation (CBC)
[6] St. Lucia Television Service (SLTV)

DE BAND: 1970-1977

Part 4

Preface

This series of seven poems on DE BAND is written with a twist of the Dominican (DA) dialect, using 'de' for 'the' and 'dey' for 'they.'

Part 4 is written to show the continuous struggles we faced as female musicians for practice space, and to highlight the growing popularity of DE BAND.

-- Rosalind Severin McClean, December 2, 2012

"Music gives a soul to the universe,
Wings to the mind,
Flight to the imagination, and
Life to everything."

-- PLATO

ENDLESS GIGS

De 1970s music era peaked
With numerous music bands
In Dominica, DA
We joined on that music beat
And gained popularity
And media attention
"De Missin' Dimensions" Band
Was a huge music explosion

More hassle for practice time
More struggle for suitable space
Still!
DE BAND in demand
More bookings to make
More gigs to take
But!
We craved
We begged for a place

Liquid Ice in session
No time for our BAND
Dey have their gigs

Dey shunned us
And boasted
But!
We aimed to find a way
Gigs rolling in
Excitement setting in
Practice, practice
But where
Was our nervous plea

De Wooden Stools Band
Cedrick, Brian Rock and de guys
Offered a space in their cellar
And allowed us use
Of their electric instruments
But on their time
We had to fit in
That tight schedule
Of de Wooden Stools Band
For shows we booked
And practice
We had to hook

Every Mother's Child Band
In de Old Cave Disco
At Roseau Bay front
With Redds, Ormond,
Albie and Nicky
Opened the way
To let us play
On their instruments
Dey flashed a chord or two
To add to our busy
Music repertoire

A booking made
At de Ham Club
Near Huitault Way
Roseau on a rapid buzz
DE BAND on favored call
Gigs coming in
Bookings tight
DE BAND in high demand

Yes!
We were chosen
To play at
De big Sunday Brunch
At de popular
Sunset Terrace Beach Club
Down Canefield Highway

That famous Beach Club
Where!
Our beautiful sea
And black volcanic sand
And radiant sunset meet

Where!
Rain and shine compete
And coconut and almond trees
Line the beach

Where!
Barbecue grills and smoke
And Dominican food and drink
And all de hang out crowd
Party in a fantastic show
And sweet disco music

We captured headlines
"De Missin' Dimensions" Band
We were exhilarated
Running up and down de stage
Getting instruments tuned
And ready for de show
Norlda got an electric shock

Rosalind took a fall
Her block heels hooked
In her blue elephant pants
But we jammed
We stunned de screaming crowds
Entertaining people
All over that beach
And in
Sunset Terrace Club

"De Missin' Dimensions" Band
The talk of the town
Seized de spotlight
In the biggest show on island
We were selected to highlight
Harlem City Stage
On Newtown Savannah
Dominica, DA
DE BAND added more girls
Aroused more of an attraction
With those extra vibes

Popo, Royette, and Anne
To add to the microphones
Creating a stormy blast
Singing those heavy hits

Of de days pop tunes
Alternate singers they were
Creating a variety of melodies
To our epic music delight

Encore was de Harlem chant
In the grand open Savannah
Under the gorgeous starry sky

Encore was the enthused chant
That sailed over the edges
With the night breeze
Where de cool mountain air
And de warm sea breeze caress

Encore was the racket chant
And we played
Again and again
We rocked that Savannah
We hit for wicket six
With our sharp
And intoxicating performance

Yes!
We made our mark
We got our crowd
We scored encore
We played music
We rocked

"De Missin' Dimensions" Band
Was *de only all-girl band*
In all of Dominica, DA land
And the Caribbean

DE BAND Members ("De Missin' Dimensions" Band):

    Rosalind Severin McClean
    Jennifer Fadelle Johnson
    Arnolda Williams Shillingford
    Ella Butler
    Jean Munro (R.I.P.)

Additional singers:
    Cecelia Piper Howard (Popo)
    Anne Williams Zamor
    Royette Valmond Russell

-- Rosalind Severin McClean, December 2, 2012

OCEANS OF THOUGHTS

DE BAND: 1970-1977

Part 5

THIS WAS HOW WE ROLLED

This is the day that the Lord has made. Let us rejoice and be glad in it. Jah is all good! Thank you, Lord for this deep inspiration of your Word, which I have been receiving to continue this journey of writing.

I am under the rock. The rock is higher that I. Jehovah Jireh, I am under the rock. Praises to the Most High for His grace. He has given to me that passion to write. It is through this order that I am continuing to present my work to my readers in this wonderful project of *Oceans of Thoughts*.

I am taking this opportunity to document the journey of "De Missin' Dimensions" Band. Although we were just a small female band of musicians exploring our musical talents, we definitely made history on the island of Dominica (DA), from 1970 to 1977. This history on DE BAND is just as important as any other history which has been documented.

I would like to brief you all on how we attained the music chords and the lyrics for the pop songs we played. We had to wait for the radio stations to play the tunes on their programs, so we could jot down whatever words we could catch. The songs were played frequently during the day, but we were in high school, so this had to wait for after school hours and on weekends.

But we caught on. Jennifer Fadelle Johnson used to call Radio Dominica (DA) to request songs. I used to sit by the radio to listen to Radio St. Kitts, and Radio Antilles in Montserrat. The other girls would do just about the same and we would bring our words together.

Jennifer and I would write our own chords for the guitar music. I wrote my chords for the piano and organ. I also had a *Leeds Guitar Dictionary 2400 Chord Positions*, and other teach-yourself chord books. We did not have music books for those songs. That was in the 1970s on the island.

There were no computers, no cell phones, no electronics to get the music at our fingertips. It was endless practicing on the piano and box guitars before we got to the electric instruments. That was how we rolled.

Part 5 of this seven-poem series is sure to take you on another leg of our fascinating journey.

One Love to all of you. Showers of blessings to all from the greatest EL-ROI. Om Santih santih santih! Peace!

-- Rosalind Severin McClean, July 12, 2019

OCEANS OF THOUGHTS

Preface

This series of seven poems on DE BAND is written with a twist of the Dominican (DA) dialect, using 'de' for the and 'dey' for they.

Part 5 is written to take you through the climb to the Dominica's (DA) Carnival stage of 1974, and also, to highlight some of our favorite hits.

Keep in mind that during that time, we were young female teenagers and musicians, bending the rules of the male ego on electric instruments on Dominica (DA) island.

-- Rosalind Severin McClean, December 2, 2012

"One good thing about music,
when it hits you, you feel no pain."

-- BOB MARLEY

CARNIVAL SEASON

"De Missin' Dimensions" Band
Now in the omphalos of its fame
Escalating with great momentum
Engaging de enraptured fans
Scaling up de music platform
Of that mid 1970s era
It was like magic
But who would have said
That DE BAND would have made
Top news in Dominica, DA

But practices still remained
To be untangled in de game
Of borrowed time and space
On electric instruments
Norlda communicated
With an agog foreman
At de Fond Cole Banana Shed
Near Fond Cole Highway
Where Naked Feet Band
Stored their music instruments

Respect and added claim
As it was in
De Banana Shed
De practice came

Our demand intensified
More pumped up
On favored ground
For the Dominica's
Number one band of
The Swingin' Stars, we knew

That call in anticipation
With great expectation
To practice to perfection
On Swingin' Stars instruments
Complements and high approval
From Swingin' Stars members
We aspired
More confident
More fastidious
More promise
We triumphed

It was worth it all
As we flew
To the Arawak Cinema
Located in the middle of
The capital Roseau
A prestigious attraction
And historical prominence
To feature at de carnival festivities
In Dominica's (DA)
Elaborate 1974 carnival season

Carnival Princess Show was a blast
'Rock The Boat' we jammed
To screaming children and
Exuberant adults alike
'Hang On Snoopy' was another hit
'Day After Day' we featured, and
'Light My Fire' was a massive hit
We rocked de fans off their feet
With our electrifying music delight
From popular radio hits
Of that magical music era

We stepped on stage
In our Indian-hippie homemade
Hand-woven embroidered shirts
And bell bottom dungaree jeans
Cool in de hippie trend
And looking flashy totality

Carnival Queen Show climax
The hit of
"De Missin' Dimensions" treat
The ultimate of our feat
Queen show 1974 was it

Lucien and Mickey
Joined in our flow
With their electric guitars
As we glowed in demand
And took control
Of that
Carnival Queen Show stage
When Norlda and Popo
Made a spotlight

We played some serious music
'RESPECT' it was for Popo and Anne
'Fire Baby, I'm On Fire' for Norlda
Oops! Norlda forgot de words

But! No one knew
Because dey took over
Rosalind, Ella, & Lucien
And brought down de house
In truth

We had a blast
Enthralled de crowd
But wait!
Jennifer in de audience
School examination time
Screamed she did
And!
A double take dey made
Folks entranced around her
For she should have been
On that Carnival stage

We attained great respect
With our successful feat
Encore we gained
With our enchanting fame
With more radio hits like
'I Shot The Sheriff' and 'She's A Lady'
'Money Money Money' and 'Kung Fu Fighting'
'Proud Mary' and 'Listen to the Music'
'Mama' and 'Jeremiah Was a Bullfrog'
And 'Ain't No Sunshine'
To name few

Yes!

We made it

We crowned our chart

We reached our goal

To star on the 1974 Carnival stage

Of Dominica's delightful

Carnival Princess Show, and

The extravagant 1974

Dominica (DA)

Carnival Queen Show

DE BAND Members ("De Missin' Dimensions" Band):

    Rosalind Severin McClean

    Jennifer Fadelle Johnson

    Arnolda Williams Shillingford

    Ella Butler

    Jean Munro (R.I.P.)

Added members:

    Cecelia Piper Howard (Popo)

    Anne Williams Zamor

    Lucien Guye

    Michael Fadelle

-- Rosalind Severin McClean, December 2, 2012

DE BAND: 1970-1977

Part 6

Praise the Lord in the mighty name of Jah who lights the path and continues to set the pace on this project, Oceans of Thoughts.

'A little more oil in my lamp keep it burning. A little more oil in my lamp I pray. A little more oil in my lamp keep it burning. Keep it burning to continue to light the path on this wonderful project of Oceans of Thoughts every day.'

Yes, keep the love flowing on this path. I reach to the good food of pure nectar to flow through the stems on this project, Oceans of Thoughts. May the good energy of the Greater Om penetrate through, and scatter whatsoever which may trifle. In the name of Jehovah Tsidkenu[7], open the stems of Oceans of Thoughts to keep it clear, and to receive only those positive energies to the rhythm of Oceans of Thoughts.

One Love and showers of blessings to all of us. Om Santih, Santih, Peace!

-- Rosalind Severin McClean, July 30, 2019

---

[7] "The Lord of righteousness" Jeremiah 23:6

Preface

This series of seven poems on *DE BAND* is written with a twist of the Dominican (DA) dialect, using 'de' for 'the' and 'dey' for 'they.'

Part 6 is written to embark the readers on the journey to two major dance halls on Dominica (DA) island in 1974, and to show how in the pinnacle of this fascinating experience, other prominent Dominican (DA) musicians eagerly assisted *DE BAND* to a tight finish.

-- *Rosalind Severin McClean, December 3, 2012*

"Beautiful music is the art of the Prophets
that can calm the agitations of the soul:
It is one of the most magnificent and delightful presents
God has given us."

-- MARTIN LUTHER

THE PINACLE

That vivacious music era of 1974
Still in a rapturous continuation
Of an amazing cultural music explosion
"De Missin' Dimensions" in full grandeur
Securing some important gigs
And booking them expeditiously

Intrigued and curious
Came young and impressionable
Shyla from India
Shocked and awestruck she was
At the sight of an all-girl band
Unstoppable we were
At the Windsor Park festival
We tantalized her
And drew more
Spellbound fans anew

Swingin' Stars took over
More practice time and
Insurmountable favor
For the vitality
Of two dance halls

De Sisserou Hotel and
De Green Grotto
In a collaboration
Edged "De Missin' Dimensons"
On Dominica's (DA) 1974
Carnival media headlines

But advertise we must fashion
Those occasions we must seize
For banner and laughter
And proud for de matter
For Dominica Green Grotto
And Dominica Sisserou Hotel
We must engage

Rumbustious motorbikes on de trail
Augg, Desmond and Marcel
Leading de motorcade
Of "De Missin' Dimensions" parade
938 Blue Bug follow
Norlda at de wheel
Horns tooting
Engines revving
We hop de bikes
Rosalind, Ella and Jean
Raising dust and calamity

En route to
Dominica (DA) Botanical Gardens
A cricket tournament at play
We made it our venture

Excitement and high esteem
For DE BAND topped the action
Dance time in the elite ballroom
The biggest party
Of Dominica (DA) carnival time
The Dominica Samedi Gras dance
At The Sisserou Hotel
To add to DE BAND
Sizzling music repertoire

"De Missin' Dimensions"
Featured in this grand debut
Whilst Swingin' Stars members
Had them to perfection
At this epic carnival celebration
In Dominica (DA) 1974

Green Grotto dance
Was the other attraction
Causing deybah with ambition
"De Missin' Dimensions" Band
Called to de stage
With an enticing mix

But forth song on de list
DE BAND
Wobbled with excitement

We got stuck
In the core
Of the Kung Fu Fighting hit
Ella in her frustration
Threw de drumsticks
Of her favorite beat
Norlda and Jean at de mic
Their nerves setting in
Clicking fingers they did
To catch an attentive spin

Rosalind on de organ
Making de keys talk
De leader must stay
Nowhere to walk
No tricks to fix
That organ must speak
Rosalind hit those music chords
On high voltage
And covered DE BAND
To score encore
Invigorating de girls
To finish de gig

Jennifer missed de boat
Rosalind almost did too
When Mr. Fadelle
And Mr. Severin vented
Grotto! No play!
Jennifer had no escape
But Rosalind had a plan
In de 938 Blue Bug
With Ella, Norlda and Jean
For it was pivotal
To the Green Grotto
Rosalind had to go

But to crown it all
We captured de 1974
Carnival street flow
When Swingin' Stars and
"De Missin' Dimensions"
Jammed to Dominica's local calypsos
On top Swingin' Stars colossal truck
Carnival revelers and bystanders
Gazed in awe along de carnival route
As they witnessed history unfold

"De Missin' Dimensions" Band
In its element
Embraced the invitation
To play music
With those great
Dominican (DA) musicians
We hit the apotheosis of
"De Missin' Dimensions" dominance

The culmination of
DE BAND carnival episode
Spiraled appreciable motivation
And incited an interest
To play again
On Swingin' Stars carnival truck
For another year or two
In favorable succession.

DE BAND ("De Missin' Dimensions" Band Members):

Rosalind Severin McClean: leader, rhythm guitar, organ & backup singer
Jennifer Fadelle Johnson: lead guitar, bass & backup singer
Arnolda Williams Shillingford: bass & lead singer
Ella Butler: drums & backup singer
Jean Munro (R.I.P.): congas

Bikers:
Desmond Green
Marcel Cruickshank (Malaway) (R.I.P.)
Augg Piper (R.I.P.)

-- Rosalind Severin McClean, December 3, 2012

DE BAND: 1970-1977

Part 7

Blessings All!

Praises and thanks to Jah, who delights in keeping the Holy Ghost energy sitting on top of this highly spirited project. "I will meditate on the glorious splendor of Your majesty, and on Your wondrous works." "You have hedged this project behind and before, and laid Your hand upon it" in the Mighty name of Jehovah Nissi.

I am very grateful for all the positive energy flowing through Oceans of Thoughts.

This has been a most fascinating experience to take the readers on this wonderful journey on memory lane, of De Missin' Dimensions Band of Dominica (DA).

I salute the Divine inspiration which sits on top Oceans of Thoughts. That lights the whole being of Oceans of Thoughts. That beams through the pure personality of Oceans of Thoughts. That bulbs highest encouragement on Oceans of Thoughts.

Jah Bless! One Love!

Om Santih Santih Santih! Peace!

-- Rosalind Severin McClean, August 18, 2019

Preface

This series of seven poems on DE BAND is written with a twist of the Dominican (DA) dialect, using 'de' for 'the' and 'dey' for 'they.'

Part 7 is written to show the readers how effective we as female musicians were on the neighboring French Media, and to emphasis how impressive we were with our creative ideas to emulate a successful Woodstock festival on Dominica (DA) island.

This also takes us to the thrilling conclusion of the 7-part poem series on DE BAND. I stay humbled and feel very encouraged from all the positive attention given to DE BAND on this wonderful project.

-- Rosalind Severin McClean, December 6, 2012

*"Music is a language that doesn't
speak in particular words.
It speaks in emotions,
and if it's in the bones,
it's in the bones."*

-- KEITH RICHARDS

THE FRENCH MEDIA AND

WOODSTOCK FESTIVAL

That mystical sparkling Milky Way
Transparent musical crescendo
With an effect so powerful
"De Missin' Dimensions" Band
Fluorescent in the waxing gibbous
Of the 1970s moon

We placed that music bar
Of that 70s decade so far
"De Missin' Dimensions'" reign soared
On exemplary curtain call
We reached our destiny bold
Come change and waning fold
DE BAND's demand so vigorous
Creating that music sound
But de nearing end
Seemed only
Just too quick

Opportunity of massive creativity
To launch at Stowe Estate
On de south seacoast
A major musical impact
Evinced and exuberant
For it was
Woodstock festival
We emulated

An imagination so clever
Inclusive and compact
With several music bands
On Dominica (DA) island
But transportation
To de country heights
We must secure
To effectuate
"De Missin' Dimensions"
Commitment

It was Mr. Fadelle again
To DE BAND's favoring rescue
With his old Bedford truck
And his avid driver
They accommodated DE BAND
In de execution
Of de enthusiastic plans

We loaded that truck
One trip to make
"De Missin' Dimensions" Band
With all electric instruments
And other ebullient fans
Journeyed to Stowe Estate

That was an ambitious undertaking
We used all cottages on de Estate
For guest and picnic and partying
No electricity at Stowe
And in that part of the island
De Stowe Estate generator
Became our greatest savior
Operating in full use
Energizing and illuminating
Our Woodstock festival
In that 1970s era
On Dominica (DA) island

French News Media
Radio Jumbo of Martinique
On Dominica at that time
Desired a major segment
In an audition
And a spirited interview
With DE BAND

De French News Reporters
Quite serious with intent
Prompted
Staunch currents of interest
To capture some fascinated
Apex music headlines

"De Missin' Dimensions" lionized
Favored approval identified
On a vast popularity plateau
We inspired de French Media
In total amazement
And in all their excitement
Invited DE BAND
To sing de long lyrics of
De Jingles commercial song
But no, DE BAND
Was not that kind of group
"De Missin' Dimensions"
Was not a singing troupe

In the epilogue
Of this great music era
At the enthused tip
Of de 1970s decade

De reign of
"De Missin' Dimensions" Band
Took a courageous dip
When work
And travel exhaled

Like the waning moon
Sitting in a radiant sunset peak
Of a Dominica scenic sky
In the summit of this
Mind-blowing experience
DE BAND members
Made a change in direction

An era so tremendous
Of music so complete
So compelling
So entertaining
So gratifying
No other girls
Followed the lead
Of "De Missin' Dimensions" Band
De only all-girl band
In all of Dominica (DA) island
And throughout de region
In this memorable
1970s music decade

"De Missin' Dimensions" Band Members:

Rosalind Severin McClean
Jennifer Fadelle Johnson
Arnolda Williams Shillingford
Ella Butler
Jean Munro (R.I.P.)

-- Rosalind Severin McClean, December 6, 2012

OCEANS OF THOUGHTS

"THE MISSIN' DIMENSIONS"! DOMINICA'S FIRST AND ONLY ALL-GIRL MUSIC BAND! & FIRST ALL-GIRL BAND IN THE REGION, 1970-1977

We started in the early 1970s when Dr. Watty called me to play guitar for his concerts, which were held at the St. Gerald's Hall. For the second show I told him to call Jennifer as well because she also played the guitar. And there the duo was born; Rosalind Severin McClean and Jennifer Fadelle Johnson on acoustic guitars.

When the nuns at the Convent High School received their electrical instruments and drums as a donation, they were in the principal's office where we could see them. That sparked our interest, so we asked to play on them. We were looking for a drummer and asked Ella Butler. Arnolda Williams Shillingford was already singing for the school. Jean Munro (R.I.P.) was always hanging out with us, so the congas were hers to play. Rosalind Severin McClean alternating between rhythm guitar and organ, and Jennifer Fadelle Johnson on lead guitar.

Rosalind "Rose" Caines LaRocque was head girl at that time, and the nuns would only allow us to use the instruments, unless she joined the group. Rose said yes, she would sing. So the Convent

High School Band was formed. The original "Missin'

Dimensions" All Girl Band was born. We were very young teenagers at that time: second, third, and fourth formers, except for Rose. We were only allowed to play religious songs on those Convent instruments, which we played at many events. But we took a chance to practice pop music in the school hall, and Sister José heard us. From then, it was all over for us with those instruments. We had to look for other ways to practice.

As time went on, we added more members, such as Cecilia "Popo" Piper Howard on organ and vocals; other vocalists like Royette Valmond Russell, Anne Williams Zamor, Chantel; and Cora Richards as drummer substitute.

When one of the guitarists was unable to play at an event, we were forced to call in male substitutes to help because there were no females available who could play. These males were Lucien Guye and Michael Fadelle. We used instruments from other bands like the Liquid Ice, The Swingin' Stars, Every Mother's Child, Wooden Stools, and not forgetting Naked Feet instruments in the Banana Shed, for practices and shows.

In those days we were not focused on getting paid as we were just excited for the opportunities to showcase our musical talents and to fulfill those numerous gigs. We were compensated, however, with food and drinks compliments of the organizers of those events.

On the third night of the Harlem City Stage Festival in 1973, we were surprised when Loftus Emanuel the event organizer paid DE BAND $86 EC[8] which was a percentage of the ticket sales. The Missin' Dimensions Band was one of the many bands in the festival and we were quite thrilled to have gotten our share.

This encouraged us even more to continue playing at numerous venues around Dominica.

-- Rosalind Severin McClean, June 1, 2016.

[8] Eastern Caribbean Currency

OCEANS OF THOUGHTS

Preface

As he walked through my door in humbled vision of a tall brown-skinned male, wrapped in a white bath towel with water running from the back of his head, dripping through his black, flat, wavy haircut, I lift the memories of some well-established musicians of Dominica and their contributions to The Missin' Dimensions Band.

I must present to you the very impressive article that I wrote on Zouk Music in the Carib News NY in April 1995, clarifying the roots of Zouk.

This was written with the permissions and presentations of two great musicians out of Dominica: Vivian Wallace of Exile One Band, and Pat Aaron of the Naked Feet Band, and with the experience and diligence of one of our accomplished calypsonians, Hayden Desiere, known as "Lord Tokyo."

This documentary has gotten the attention of numerous fans.

-- Rosalind Severin McClean, May 1, 2021

"Music in the soul
Can be heard by the universe."

-- LAO TZU

"ZOUK MUSIC": ITS ROOTS

I wrote this article on Zouk music in response to an erroneous assertion that Zouk is Haitian music and Kassav is a Haitian band. My article was published in the NY Carib News Week Ending on April 4th, 1995. Some people are still very confused as to the origin of Zouk music.

The roots of Zouk music come from the island of the Commonwealth of Dominica, West Indies. Zouk originated from Cadance-lypso music which was created by Exile One of Dominica.

To quote Vivian Wallace, original bassist for Exile One:

"In 1973, a group of young Dominican musicians (Oliver Cruickshank on drums; Julie Mourillon, vocals/guitar; Fitzroy Williams, vocals/keyboard; Gordon Henderson, leader/vocals/organ; Cremlin Fingal, trumpet/vocals; and myself on bass/vocals) got together to form Exile One. Brian Rock was with the group but could not continue as he was of a younger age.

"We created a type of creole music called Cadance-lypso. From Cadance came our Zouk. In those days, there were no recording studios in Dominica, so we moved to Guadeloupe to record our songs. From there we moved to France."

Vivian continues: "The first Zouk song ever made was called 'Dominique-ki-dou' which means 'Sweet Dominica.'"

In the book World of Creole, written by Josélyn Guildbaud, about the history of Zouk in Dominica, the reader can gain some valuable information about the history of Dominica's music and the numerous live bands on the island, including Exile One, Midnight Groovers and Grammacks, to name a few. Vivian says, "Cadance and Zouk music have made the charts in Europe. Exile One is very well known in Europe and among the French and Creole Caribbean islands."

On the contrary, Compas is Haitian music. As Vivian says: "We like and respect the types of music Haiti has. As a matter of fact, at Dominican parties, Compas is very much appreciated. Zouk is played by Haitian bands as well."

Another artist out of Dominica, Jahlee, said at that time that she was focusing on Zouk for her new album because Zouk is something of our own. Kassav is a live band from the French island of Guadeloupe and not from Haiti. Kassav has also been in the forefront with Zouk music.

The core members of Kassav came from the group Les Vikings, a popular Guadeloupian band which also provided back-up Cadence music for Ophelia Olivacee of Dominica in the 1970s and early 1980s. Ophelia has had as much success in the French West Indies and Europe as Exile One and Grammacks. In 1981 she won the Maracas d'Or (Golden Maracas), a prestigious award given to Black artists in France.

Jeff Joséph, formerly of Grammacks, must also be mentioned for his outstanding contribution to Zouk music.

Dominica's Cadance influenced not only Zouk music, but also helped foster calypso's evolution into Soca music. Soca music began when Lord Shorty of Trinidad went to Dominica in the early 1970s to promote his album. It was there that Dominican local calypsonian Lord Tokyo

(Hayden Desiere) penned the creole chorus for Lord Shorty's hit song "Ou dit mwen ou petit Shorty, ou dit mwen ou petit ou marti" (You say you were small Shorty, but you lied). The first Soca song started as a collaboration between Shorty and Tokyo.

According to Lord Tokyo, the bassline for the song came from the Swinging Stars band of Dominica, and the beat from Cadance-lypso. Herrie Etienne, a Dominican, was the bass player for Swinging Stars at that time. Soca was born out of a combination of Calypso and Cadence, hence the name SO-CA.

About the same time in 1975, some members of Charlie's Roots, Shadow, and drummer Erol Wise, among others, expressed interest in Cadance when they visited K H Studios in Trinidad, where Naked Feet band of Dominica was recording an album.

Pat Aaron, original bassist and leader of Naked Feet, remembers that these artists came to the recording sessions at the studio to listen to, and to be inspired by, the Cadence beat which stimulated new ideas. Calypso was at the time searching for new ground. This was around the time that Maestro, one of calypso's most versatile and innovative artists, just approaching the peak of his career, succumbed to a fatal hit-and-run car accident.

These facts are just being pointed out to clarify the roots of Zouk, Cadence and Soca music, and the fact that many times, great things come from humble beginnings and thus, it is usually the trumpeters and not the innovators or the creators who receive the recognition.

Written by Rosalind Severin McClean © March 1995

All rights reserved.

OCEANS OF THOUGHTS

Blossoming in harmonious cluster

Incense lilies of life

Chaudiere Pool in Bense, Dominica

Emerald Pool, Dominica

The Boeri Lake– (Roseau Valley, Dominica)

The Boiling Lake, Dominica

Beautiful rugged coastline of Dominica

My treasured guitar chord book from 1970

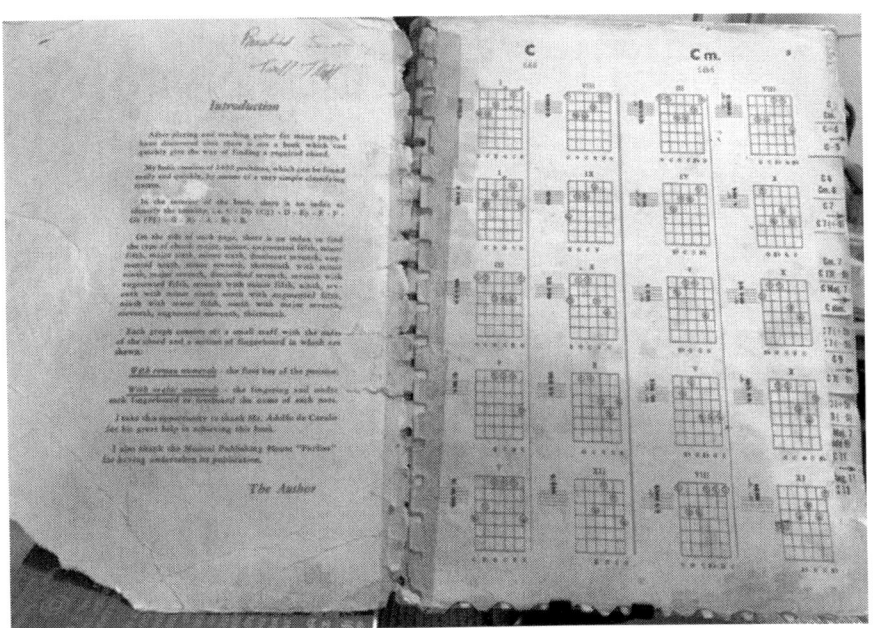

Introduction to Leeds Guitar Dictionary

The "Missin' Dimensions" Band, 1973

Practicing at the Banana Shed on Naked Feet

Band Instruments in Fond Cole

Jean Munro, Arnolda Williams, Ella Butler,

Cecilia "Popo" Piper, Rosalind Severin

Rosalind Severin, 1975

Leader, organist, rhythm guitarist, back-up singer

Rosalind Severin, 1975

Leader, organist, rhythm guitarist, back-up singer

Jennifer Fadelle, 1973

Lead Guitarist, back-up singer

Arnolda Williams, 1973

Bassist, lead vocals

Ella Butler, 1971

Drummer, back-up singer

Jean Munro, 1980s

Congas

Liquid Ice Band, featuring Arnolda and Popo

Arawak Cinema, 1974

Michael "Mikey" Fadelle, of Liquid Ice Band

Arawak Cinema, 1974

Tony Valmond, of Liquid Ice Band, 1970s

Every Mother's Child Band, Sunset Terrace Beach Club, 1971:
Albie Frampton, Francis Casimir and Nicholas Casimir.
Ormond Charlmers, Gairy Dedier and Julie Mourillon joined later.
Among the guys: Anison Rabess of Voltage 4 Band, Arnolda and
Jennifer of the "Missin' Dimensions"

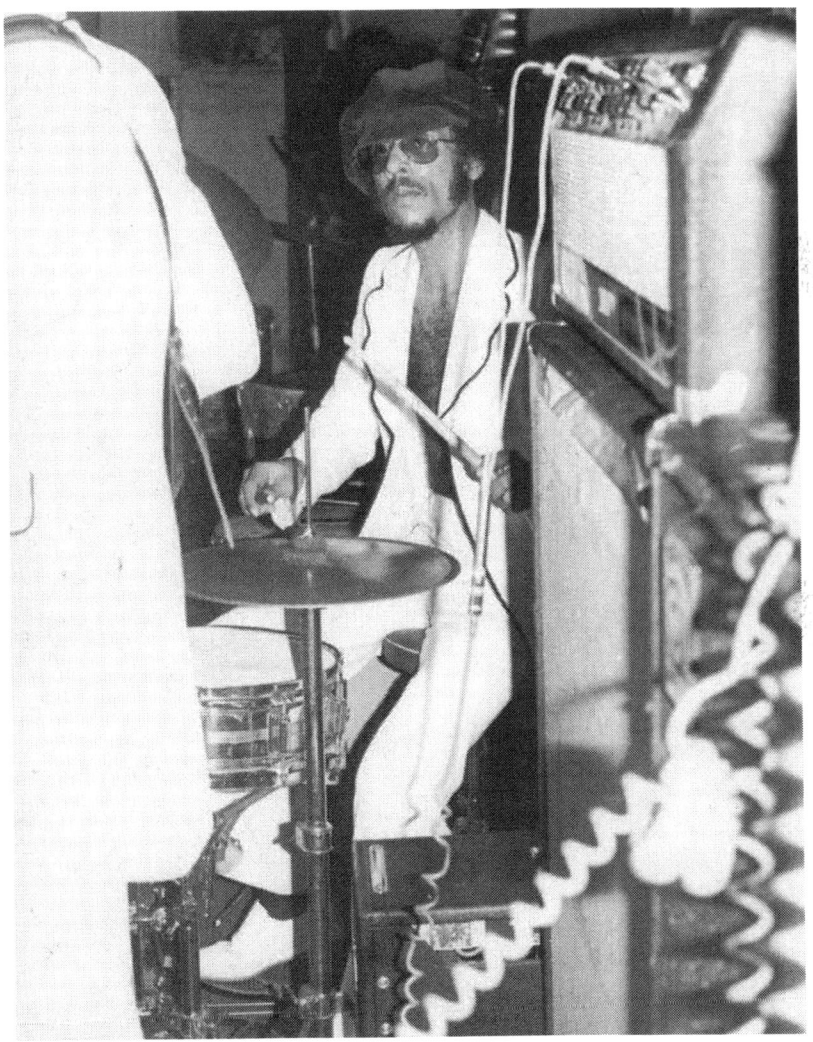

Oliver Cruickshank, of Voltage 4 Band, 1970s

938 Blue Bug with Arnolda, 1972

(The "Missin' Dimensions" favored car rides.)

Arnolda's Birthday Celebration, 1975:

Rosalind, Jennifer, Ella, her sister Annette and other friends

The "Missin' Dimensions" Motorcade, 1974:

Worrel Hurtault and Bonifast Winston;

and

Marcel (Malaway) Cruickshank, of Swingin' Stars Orchestra

Desmond Green, 1974

"Missin' Dimensions" Motorcade

Exile One Band, 1973:

Gordon Henderson, Oliver Cruickshank, Julie Mourillon, Vivian
Wallace, Fitzroy Williams, and Cremlin Fingal.

(Featured Article: "ZOUK MUSIC": ITS ROOTS)

Vivian Wallace, Bassist

Wooden Stools Band and Exile One Band, 1973

Brian (Rocket) Rock with Dominican friends & musicians in Moja Nya Band in New York, 1979.
(Bruce Norris' first gig was in 1972 with Rocket and Sty Larocque in Dominica, at the 1st Harlem Jam Festival, Newtown Savannah.)

Brian Rock, 2001

The Swingin' Stars Orchestra, 1978
(Norman Letang and his musicians who had the "Missin'
Dimensions" Band to perfection
at the epic Carnival celebrations in 1974; (with Phillip
Horsford and Levi Loblack on vocals)

The "Missin' Dimensions" Reunion:

Rosalind Severin McClean, Jennifer Fadelle Johnson,

Arnolda Williams Shillingford

Lunch at La Robe Creole Restaurant, Roseau, Dominica, 1986

Cecilia Piper Howard and Jennifer Fadelle Johnson in Dominica, 2017

Ella Butler in Dominica, 2018

Arnolda Williams Shillingford in Bermuda, 2019

Rosalind Severin McClean and daughter Malti

McClean in New York, 2019

"...As the ripples formed by a pebble
Thrown in a pool keep widening
Until they reach the distant shores."

-- MR. STANLEY FADELLE, DOMINICA

ABOUT THE AUTHOR

Rosalind Severin McClean, best-selling author of *Oceans of Thoughts: Book One*, is known for her profound and most inspiring writing style. Her impressive work in poetry has claimed excellent reviews from her many audiences, both local and international. Not only has she participated in Open Mic events and written editions in newspaper articles to showcase her work, but she is also an exemplary performer in the arts, dance, and culture.

Born in The Commonwealth of Dominica to Mr. & Mrs. Clifford A. Severin, Ms. McClean lives with her daughter Malti McClean in Queens, New York.

NOTES

Made in the USA
Middletown, DE
24 February 2022